Hacking Fashion: Fleece

Summit Free Public Library

CHERRY LAKE PUBLISHING • ANN ARBOR, MICHIGAN

by Kristin Fontichiaro

Cherry Lake
Publishing

A Note to Adults: Please review the instructions for the activities in this book before allowing children to do them. Be sure to help them with any activities you do not think they can safely complete on their own.

A Note to Kids: Be sure to ask an adult for help with these activities when you need it. Always put your safety first!

Published in the United States of America by Cherry Lake Publishing
Ann Arbor, Michigan
www.cherrylakepublishing.com

Series Editor: Kristin Fontichiaro
Photo Credits: Cover and pages 1, 5, 14, 27, and 32, ©Regents of the University of Michigan; page 4, ©Lara604/tinyurl.com/m5n848x/CC-BY-2.0; pages 9, 11, 13, 18, 19, 20, 21, 22, 24, 25, and 28, ©Kristin Fontichiaro

Library of Congress Cataloging-in-Publication Data
Fontichiaro, Kristin.
  Hacking fashion. Fleece / by Kristin Fontichiaro.
    pages cm. — (21st century skills innovation library. Makers as innovators)
  Audience: Grade 4 to 6.
  Includes index. ISBN 978-1-63362-376-7 (lib. bdg.) —
ISBN 978-1-63362-404-7 (pbk.) — ISBN 978-1-63362-432-0 (pdf) —
ISBN 978-1-63362-460-3 (e-book)
1. Clothing and dress—Remaking—Juvenile literature. 2. Fleece (Textile)—Juvenile literature. 3. Fabric flowers—Juvenile literature. I. Title. II. Title: Fleece.
  TT550.F658 2016
  746.9'2—dc23   2015004863

Cherry Lake Publishing would like to acknowledge the work of the Partnership for 21st Century Skills. Please visit www.p21.org for more information.

Printed in the United States of America
Corporate Graphics
July 2015

Contents

Chapter 1 **What Is Hacking? What Is Fleece?** 4

Chapter 2 **Scarves** 9

Chapter 3 **Keep Your Head Warm!** 17

Chapter 4 **Mitten Magic** 23

Chapter 5 **Pom-poms and Flowers** 27

Glossary 30

Find Out More 31

Index 32

About the Author 32

Chapter 1

What Is Hacking?
What Is Fleece?

What do you do when you outgrow your clothes or get tired of wearing the same thing over and over? Maybe you give it to a younger sibling or donate it to a thrift store. Some people turn worn-out clothing into rags for cleaning or for working on their cars. Others simply throw their old clothes in the trash.

You probably have some old clothes in your closet that you don't wear anymore.

Old clothing can be turned into all kinds of fun new things to wear.

There's something else you can do with clothes that are no longer needed. You can cut them up and create something new out of them. This is called hacking fashion. When most people think of hacking, they think of breaking into computers. However, hacking can mean something else, too. To hack something means to change it to meet your needs. When you hack fashion, you take something you don't need and turn it into something you do need. Along the way, you make one-of-a-kind clothing you can use to create a unique look.

When **makers** hack fashion, they look at clothing differently. They don't just see what's already there. They

Gathering Supplies

You will need a few supplies to complete the projects in this book:

- Some **secondhand** fleece tops and pants
- A sharp pair of sewing scissors or pinking shears
- Trim material such as rickrack, lace, or ribbon
- A washable pen or marker with dark ink
- A fabric tape measure
- Buttons and beads
- Thread and needles
- Sewing machine (optional)
- Hair elastic

You will not need a clothes iron. In fact, you should never use an iron when working with fleece. The plastic in the fleece will melt and stick to your iron! Never use fleece for making hot pads or oven mitts, either—melt-o-rama!

see possibilities for what the fabric could be turned into. A maker might see an old pullover and ask, "What if I cut it down the middle and made it into a jacket?" Or, "What if I cut rings across the front? Could I fringe this part? Add a patch here? Shorten this **hem**?" Makers might see a long-sleeved shirt and imagine cutting the sleeves for a short-sleeved look for warmer weather. Imagining your future **garment** is a big part of the fun.

In this book, we'll look at projects made out of polar fleece. What's polar fleece? Well, it's not a natural fiber like cotton or wool. Those fabrics come from plants and animals. Polar fleece (or just fleece, for short) is made from plastic. Sometimes it even comes from recycled soda bottles! Because it's plastic, polar fleece is lightweight, doesn't absorb water, and dries quickly. It also keeps your body warm in cold weather. Fleece isn't only useful. It's also soft and fuzzy, so it feels good against your skin. It comes in a lot of different colors, too.

Fleece is used to make jackets, hats, mittens, pullovers, and even pajama pants! You can find fleece garments at almost any kind of clothing store. Even some grocery stores and drugstores have a rack of fleece garments on display.

Just as plastic brings some benefits to polar fleece fabric, it also causes some problems. Because fleece is not a natural fiber, it is not **biodegradable**. This means if people throw out their fleece when they're done wearing it, those discarded garments could be stuck in a landfill forever. When you turn used secondhand fleece garments into new creations, you extend the useful life of the fabric. This helps the environment by keeping potential trash out of landfills.

Fleece is easy to work with if you have a sharp pair of scissors. Its ends won't fray when you wash it. Best of all, there is a lot of polar fleece available in secondhand shops and thrift stores and at garage sales. These garments often cost as little as a dollar each, which is much cheaper than buying fleece in a fabric store. Check in the children's, men's, and women's sections for fleece pullovers, jackets, bathrobes, and pajama pants. When you have a choice, get the largest sizes possible. These garments have the most fabric in them that you can reuse.

Try to get several garments. When you're teaching yourself to hack, you might have a project that doesn't turn out quite perfectly the first time. It's nice to just reach for another garment and start over instead of waiting for someone to take you to the store. Extra garments also mean that you'll have plenty of fabric to share if a friend comes over.

Wash secondhand garments in hot water before you use them. Try skipping the dryer and hanging the damp fleece garments on hangers or over your shower rod to dry. Because they are made of plastic, they dry very quickly.

Chapter 2

Scarves

When your grandparents were kids, they stayed warm in cold weather by wearing knit scarves around their necks. These scarves were usually made out of wool, and wool is scratchy! Today's kids are more likely to have fleece scarves. They are just as warm but are cuddly instead of itchy. Scarves are a perfect project for beginning fashion hackers because sewing is optional. The most important tool is a pair of scissors!

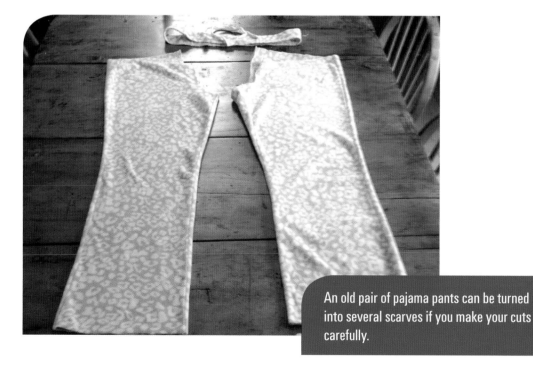

An old pair of pajama pants can be turned into several scarves if you make your cuts carefully.

Buy the Right Material

To get started, you'll need to cut scarves from your fleece garments. Fleece pajama pants are popular holiday gifts, so it is easy to find old ones at thrift shops. Be sure to look at both the inside and outside of the pants before you buy them. You want a pair that doesn't look worn out on the inside where the fabric rubbed against the wearer's body.

Remove the Waistband, but Keep It!

Now, you're ready to cut! First, you need to remove the waistband of the pants. Don't throw it away, though. Makers always hold on to leftover supplies for future projects.

Cut Off the Hem

The hem of a pair of pants is the part at the very bottom, by the ankle, where the fabric folds up and underneath itself. Cut all the way around both hems to remove them.

Cut the Scarves

Lay out the pants on a large kitchen or dining table. You'll notice that you can only lay one leg out flat

Make your cuts as straight as possible as you remove the seams.

at a time. Cut a long rectangle along the leg's side **seams**—reach all the way to the top and bottom of the pant leg. Repeat with the other pant leg. You'll end up with four scarves made from each pair of pants.

What Can You Make from Waistbands and Hems?

Members of the Michigan Makers group brainstormed some ideas for reusing waistbands and hems from old fleece pants. Can you make one of these with your leftovers?

- Belt
- Bracelet
- Stretchy elastic to wrap around a school planner and keep things from falling out
- Hair elastic or headband
- Dog collar
- Strap to hold the lid closed on a board game box
- Stretchy elastic to hold bags in place on a garbage can so they don't slip
- Key chain wristlet
- Cat toy

You can use a long ruler or yardstick to mark straight cutting lines, or you can just eyeball it as best you can. After all, your scarf will be wrapped around your neck, so nobody will know if it is crooked or not!

You'll end up with some leftover pieces along the pants' seams. Hang on to them if they are large enough. You can use them later to add patches, pom-poms, flowers, designs, fringe, pockets, and more to your designs. Discard the smaller pieces.

Pullovers work just as well as pants for making scarves.

Another Method

Don't have pajama pants? No problem! You can also make scarves from a fleece pullover. Cut across the pullover from the bottom of one armpit to the bottom of the other. Set aside the piece with the sleeves and neck hole. This should leave you with a wide loop of fabric.

Try making scarves in many different patterns and colors.

Cut off the bottom hem. Now cut that wide loop into two narrower loops. Cut each loop open by trimming off one of the seams. Use a sewing machine or sew the two strips together by hand. You can either make a really long scarf or attach the two strips together at both ends, which will make an infinity-style scarf that wraps twice around your neck for extra warmth.

Customize Your Scarves with Scissors

Now the fun begins! You might want to use scissors to customize your scarf. Do you want to cut slits into the ends of your scarf to make fringe? Tie two pieces of fringe together to make a series of knots? Cut curved edges all the way around the scarf? Create an interesting pattern by cutting shapes out of the center of the scarf? It's up to you. You can measure out each cut and mark it with chalk or a marker, or you can just eyeball it.

Some scarves wrap around the neck and are held in place with a button. You can make a scarf like this, too! Start by wrapping the scarf around your neck to see where your button should go. Use a piece of chalk or a marker to mark the spot where the two ends overlap. Take off the scarf and cut a slit where you made your mark. Make it the same width as the button you want to use. Now you have a simple buttonhole! Put the scarf back on, wrapping it around your neck so the buttonhole is on top. Reach your chalk or marker through the buttonhole to mark where the button goes. Sew the button onto this mark. Now you have a buttoned scarf!

Customizing Your Scarves with Add-ons

Now is the time to pull out your scrap fleece and trim materials. You could cut out a patch from a different color of fleece and stitch it on using a running stitch (to learn how, see http://bit.ly/runningstitch) or a sewing machine. If you leave the patch open on one side, you've added a pocket. Be sure to keep your stitches small and close together so nothing can fall out between the stitches!

You could stitch rows of lace or ribbon onto the scarf's ends or add buttons in a decorative pattern. Just make sure that the part of your scarf that will touch your neck has no hard or pointy parts—such as buttons—that would make it uncomfortable against your skin.

Chapter 3

Keep Your Head Warm!

Now that you've made a scarf, let's try something a little bit more challenging. How about a hat? Fleece hats are warm. If it's a really snowy day, they also dry quickly. This means they are comfortable to put on again just a few hours after you were outside. Start by gathering some long-sleeved fleece pullovers in colors that will complement your coat or those of your friends and family.

The Five-Minute Hat

Let's start with a really easy no-sew hat. Cut the sleeve off of a fleece garment. Pull it over your head until it fits snugly, then have a friend very carefully mark a line around your head with pins (or with a washable marker made for fabric) where the edge should be. Take off the hat and make another line of pins (or marker) 3 inches (7.6 centimeters) away from the original line. Make sure the second line you make is closer to the shoulder

This type of hat is very quick and easy to make.

seam than to the wrist of the sleeve. If you measure in the wrong direction, your hat will be too small.

Cut along the second line and fold up the 3-inch (7.6 cm) part to make a cuff. Wrap a hair tie around the wrist end of the sleeve to gather up the top of the hat into a poof. Use scissors to cut off any extra fabric. Try using pinking shears, which make zigzag cuts, for a decorative detail. Add a pom-pom or flower to decorate, or hold the hat's cuff up with a decorative badge or fashion pin.

The Easy-Sew Hat

For this project, we'll use an existing hat as a **template**. Place the hat so that an edge lines up with the bottom hem of a fleece pullover. Trace around it, making your line about 1 inch (2.5 cm) bigger than the existing hat. You can always make your new hat smaller, but never bigger, so start with a larger hat and make it smaller if you need to.

Cut through both layers of the pullover so you have two hat-shaped pieces. Flip them so that the

Start by tracing the shape of a hat you already have.

Make an Ear Band!

Use a fabric tape measure—which you can buy in sewing and crafts stores—to measure the distance around your head. Make sure the tape fits snugly around your ears as you measure.

Write down the total distance around your head.

Add 1 inch (2.5 cm) to this length. This will be the length of your ear band.

Cut a long piece of fleece that is the length you measured and about 7 inches (18 cm) wide.

Fold the fleece in half so it is about 3.5 inches (9 cm) wide. Sew along the raw edges. If you are using a sewing machine, pull gently on the fabric to stretch it as you go. If you don't do this, the thread could break when you stretch the finished ear band to put it on your head. Use loose but small stitches if you are sewing by hand. Turn the ear band right side out when you are done sewing. Tuck one end into the other and stitch it closed.

Try on the ear band. If it's too loose, trim off the seam you just made and try again.

Decorate your ear band with buttons or trim, or add flowers or pom-poms (see chapter 5 for instructions).

Chapter 4

Mitten Magic

Now that you've practiced cutting two layers of fabric at once and using some basic sewing techniques, you're ready to make a simple pair of mittens.

Fold some fleece so that it has two layers and your hand fits easily onto it. Repeat for the other hand.

Stretch your fingers apart a little bit and stretch your thumb as wide as possible. You will want to be able to move your fingers while you are wearing these mittens, so you need to allow some extra room. Trace loosely around your hand with a washable marker. Remember our rule of thumb (no pun intended!): you can always make your mitten smaller, but never bigger, so draw your line about 1 inch (2.5 cm) bigger than your actual hand. Keep your line nice and wide around your wrist. Your hand needs to fit through the wrist opening. If it is too tight, your mittens won't be wearable. Keep the cuffs of the mittens nice and long. You want to be able to tuck the finished mitten into your sleeves.

Now cut out both layers of each mitten.

You can turn these inside out and hide the seam, but cutting them around the edge with zigzags (using pinking shears) and letting the seams show can be more comfortable to wear and make a more unique fashion creation!

Use a running stitch or a sewing machine stitch of your choice to sew around the mitten. Don't sew the wrist opening shut!

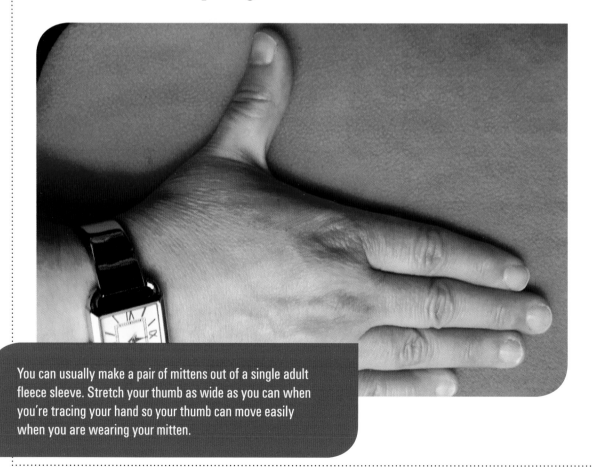

You can usually make a pair of mittens out of a single adult fleece sleeve. Stretch your thumb as wide as you can when you're tracing your hand so your thumb can move easily when you are wearing your mitten.

This mitten shows a lot of decorating techniques: sewing on trim, hand-sewing a patch, and adding a button. But the creator made a big mistake—she didn't try on her mitten to test it before she decorated it. Can you see how stubby the thumb part is? That won't be comfortable to wear! Make sure you stretch your thumb outward so you get a nice deep pocket for your thumb to sit in.

Try on the first mitten to make sure it fits. If the wrist is too tight or too short, use this mitten as a template, but make the wrist opening wider or longer. If your thumb can't move, try sewing a deeper dip between the thumb and index finger.

Once the fit is just how you like it, customize your mittens! Use hand stitching to add trim, buttons, or lace. Ask someone you know to teach you some easy **embroidery** stitches, or use running stitches to create a pattern on top of your mittens. Don't decorate the palm side, or you won't be able to grip things!

If you have sparkly buttons, can you make them look like your mitten is wearing a ring or bracelet? Can you cut scraps of fleece and hand sew them on to represent your favorite sport? What would it look like if you used a different color of fleece for the top of your mitten and a different color for the palm side? Experiment until you have made some one-of-a-kind mitts!

Electrifying Mittens!

Stores like SparkFun.com and Adafruit.com sell **conductive** thread. This is thread that conducts electricity. Sew many stitches on top of each other to make a little patch of conductive thread in the index finger and thumb area of your mittens. This will allow your mittens to conduct electricity from your fingers to a touch screen. Now you can use your phone or tablet without taking off your mittens!

Chapter 5

Pom-poms and Flowers

f you've done all the other projects in the book so far, you probably have a lot of fleece scraps by now. Makers never waste scraps, so let's make some bonus items!

Pom-poms

Pom-poms are round balls made of yarn. To make one out of fleece, cut out a long rectangle that is about 14 inches (35.5 cm) by 3 inches (7.6 cm). You can

Even your scraps can be useful for creating new projects.

make bigger or smaller pom-poms, but this is a good starter size. Cut the rectangle into little fleece strips about 0.5 inches (1.3 cm) wide and 3 inches (7.6 cm) tall. Gather them into a pile and wrap them with a piece of sturdy thread or embroidery floss about 14 inches (35.5 cm) long. Tie the thread or floss into a firm knot. This will pull the strips tightly together. (Try to get a friend to help you—you need to pull tight!) Fluff the strips into a ball and trim if needed.

Pom-poms can be used to decorate almost anything you can think of.

One Color or Many!

Pom-poms and flowers look good when you use all one color of fleece. You could make a blue pom-pom or a purple flower. But you can also mix up colors. Who says your pom-pom can't be five different shades of blue fleece? Or that your flower shouldn't be a riot of orange, purple, green, and yellow? Use your scraps and your imagination to see what looks good!

Fleece Flowers

These flowers are made from layers of fleece cut freehand (without a pattern). Start by making a small, puffy flower shape. Next, cut one that is a little bit bigger, then another one that is still bigger. Place them so the smallest is on the bottom and the largest is on top. If you'd like more layers, keep adding! Sew through the centers. Pull the thread tight so the flower puffs up around the stitches. Finally, use fabric glue or more stitches to attach your flower to a garment.

Now that you have worked through some ways to hack discarded fleece and reimagine it into simple creations, try letting your imagination run wild.

The best part about hacking fashion is knowing there's more than one way to make cool stuff!

Glossary

biodegradable (bye-oh-di-GRAY-duh-buhl) able to be broken down by natural processes

conductive (kuhn-DUHK-tiv) capable of allowing heat, electricity, or sound to pass through

embroidery (em-BROI-duh-ree) the art of sewing a picture or a design onto cloth using different colors of thread or yarn

garment (GAHR-muhnt) a piece of clothing

hem (HEM) an edge of material that has been folded over and sewn down

makers (MAY-kurz) people who use their creativity to make something

seams (SEEMZ) lines of sewing that join two pieces of material

secondhand (SEK-uhnd-hand) owned, worn, or used by someone else before you

template (TEM-plit) a shape or pattern that you draw or cut around to make the same shape in another material

Find Out More

BOOKS

Fontichiaro, Kristin. *Hacking Fashion: T-Shirts.* Ann Arbor, MI: Cherry Lake Publishing, 2015.

Kerr, Sophie. *A Kid's Guide to Sewing: 16 Fun Projects You'll Love to Make & Use—Learn to Sew with Sophie & Her Friends.* Lafayette, CA: C&T Publishing/FunStitch Studio, 2013.

WEB SITES

Instructables
http://instructables.com
Enter the search term "fleece" to find instructions for lots of sewing projects.

The Renegade Seamstress
https://chicenvelopements.wordpress.com/
Let the Renegade Seamstress help you reshape and refashion old clothing.

Index

drying, 8

ear bands, 22
embroidery stitches, 25–26

flowers, 29

hacking, 5–6
hats
    customizing, 18, 21, 22
    cutting, 18, 19, 20–21
    easy-sew hat, 19–21
    five-minute hat, 17–18
    marking, 17–18, 19
    sewing, 20

sizing, 17–18, 19
sleeves as, 17
template, 19

landfills, 7

makers, 5–6
Michigan Makers group, 12
mittens
    conductive thread, 26
    customizing, 25–26
    cutting, 24
    marking, 23
    sewing, 24, 25–26
    sizing, 23, 25

polar fleece, 7–8
pom-poms, 27–28, 29

running stitches, 15–16, 20, 24, 26

scarves
    buttons, 15, 16
    customizing, 14–16
    cutting, 10–12, 13–14
    hem removal, 10, 14
    infinity-style, 14
    leftover pieces, 12
    marking, 12
    pajama pants as, 10–12
    patches, 15–16
    pockets, 16
    pullovers as, 13–14
    sewing, 14, 15–16

About the Author

Kristin Fontichiaro teaches at the University of Michigan, where she runs the Michigan Makers makerspace project. On snow days, you can find her at home, hacking fashion.